Dark Whistle
POEMS
¤¤¤¤¤¤¤¤¤¤¤¤

Dark Whistle

POEMS

¤ ¤ ¤ ¤ ¤ ¤ ¤ ¤ ¤ ¤ ¤ ¤ ¤ ¤ ¤ ¤

By TOM WATSON

Kirkcaldy: AKROS 1997

First Published 1997
AKROS PUBLICATIONS
33 Lady Nairn Avenue
Kirkcaldy, Fife
Scotland

© copyright Tom Watson 1997
Typeset by Emtext [Scotland]
Printed and bound in Scotland
by Inglis Allen, Kirkcaldy
A CIP Record for this book
is available from the British Library

ISBN 0 86142 072 1

The publisher acknowledges subsidy
from the Scottish Arts Council
towards the publication of this volume.

CONTENTS

¤ ¤ ¤ ¤ ¤ ¤ ¤ ¤ ¤ ¤ ¤ ¤

	page
Tomorrow, Tomorrow	7
Folk Dance	8
Work Ethic	9
Slow March	10
Gluttony	11
Black Canticle	12
Therapy 1	14
Therapy 2	14
Therapy 3	15
Therapy 4	16
October Rituals	17
The Guru	18
Sources	19
Regret	20
Miss Brown De Clare	21
The Legacy	22
Four Worlds	23
Deer	24
Gulls	25
Ruminant	26
Freewill	27
Reflections	28
Long View	29
Things Athwart	30
Sad Tale	31
Thin Commitment	32
The Killing Yard	33
Camouflage	34
Against Prevailing Winds	35
Past Futures	36
Winter's Grip	36
The Apprentice	37
Frozen Moments	38

Flat Rates   39
Three New Zealand Poems:
   Night Creek   40
   What Steal?   40
   Billy Boy   41
Dealer   42
Cynic   43
Variety   44
Seeking West   45
The Optimist   46
Cat's Paw   47
Cowboy Star   48
Remembered Beeb   49
An Old Thespian Prepares   50
Early Start   51
Fragments   52
Herts 'n' Roses   53
Auld Nick Abune   54
Auld Nick Ablow   55
Wee Andy Britain   56
Ice Pantomime   56
"Bogey" Hits Cam'slang   57
Dirty Diamonds   58
Auchinleck Inheritance   59
East Neuk   60
Hotel Fairytale   61
Night Owls   62
Ancient and Modern   63
Lapis Lazu   64
Daurk Whistle   65
Bad Neebors   66
Cavity Song   67
Enclosures   68

TOMORROW, TOMORROW

Beyond immediate scan,
Through all the liquid shades,
One shadow firmer moved
In pain, aghast. A random
Stickman, shiver of a stickman
Tight in twigs and cobwebs.
He had a purse of bargains,
Pipes that sounded dawn
At dusk, was neither quick
Nor slow but like a river
Over gravel that
In confluence finds the flow.
Revered and feared this shadow
Closing deals, this opener
Of gates.

Through all the woods
The dry mice squeaked and ran.

FOLK DANCE

As shadows crossing pools of light
Or on a darkening mirror, so the motes
That danced along steel palisades
Disclosed then hid black guns.

The circle of the dancers turning, spinning
Was all rim, a sort of madness spun them
Round and out 'til only rims remained.

Old judges barked in vain as low men
Prowled the hubs, blankets for blows,
Their children doomed as labour for their lusts.

Not all were bad, some held, some died:
The ancient, unsealed roads were dark as vandals
Sacked two thousand years of greed.

Old wheels were precious, walled in ghettos,.
Music somehow made a mark
And "Ullman's Number Three for Strings"

Was threaded down, deep down, way down the gut.
The music hung and lived, the art of living
Was in dying just as frugally as possible.

Time's a very massive stone to roll,
And none of this was born before the Chemist crawled.
Now all of it exists as glintings in the sand,

In factories of glass behind men's brows
So all that can be thought can now be done:
Is fit for rescue. According to the voice print.

WORK ETHIC

There is wrong-doing, certainly
to dispassionate eyes at least,
but from my blue eyes to brown or black,
from my white eyes that focus through
your rivers, woods, your thoughts if that's
amenable to all who've gathered
here today to work,

Of course there's pain and longing but
they must be hidden underneath
our macho "hard word" barriers,
our marching feet. Somebody must
plant trees, lay tracks, lay down
responsibilities, wave through
passing goods trains?

White eyes—death eyes,
barriers—blue birches,
random—hard to focus,
easy focus on our tasks—yes?
Blue birch trees, haze, opaque,
death, burning? — is there burning? —
let's all just take things easy—uh?

Out of focus, we can burn
and burn at will before the frost
nips in to kill—I do not hear
approval. Let's have style—burn
and smile, burn and smile.

SLOW MARCH

Fire, music, rhythm,
for ages there they lay,
ashes strewn indifferently,
unnoticed every day.

All the singers singing
underwater in the tow,
all the drummers drumming
closely muffled far below.

Ice flows crushed the roses,
the seasons hung absurd,
the cracking of the North star
never tested—never heard.

All those carols cloistered
all the choristers coerced
to sing the blood of progress
no performance, all rehearsed.

According to the sky-hole,
they had much time to prepare
yet they kept their cities blazing,
through their utmost, dark despair.

GLUTTONY

Within our hollow, sea-scooped hand
Our snails devour themselves.
Circuits breed in circuits,
Our rainbows are all bled
The coloured loops are fed,
Galaxies gleam sixpence small
In our black, bedabbled halls.

Blind haar rolls in, fingering our land,
Swallowing the silver trails
That from quadrillion births
Breached waves and salty muds
To shape and tense and grain
A silver cell, a brain,
From random deep-green cauls.

Bizarre despair now webs the air.
Scientists know how quick
The sucking foot can kick
To flight on clockwork wings,
Yet whirring woodcock springs
Can never spring so far
But a feather streaked with silver falls.

BLACK CANTICLE

Little groovy hands like
Larkspurs on the coverlet,
Little groovy feet
All starry in the yard,
My Clara in the mornings,
Delicate as kittens,
Pretending to be growly
In the night.

Within the stone a frog,
Within a frog the blood,
And the cows with their crowns
Of woven leaves
Rubbing their flanks on the
Skeletal trees
While the wires all sing their song.

Her days were filled
With gardens,
Bright colours bridged
Her dawns,
All the fields around her
Grew and sang.
You hardly heard the whistle
Of the trains.

Within the frog a stone,
Within a stone the blood,
And the cows with their crowns
Of eidelweiss
Trapeze to the meadow of
Burning ice;
And the wires still sing their song.

One day the sun was shadowed,
Dark hornings brassed the sky,
In ocean eyes
The larkspurs died
The mourners sang the ancient psalm-
Notes—why?
The song is always—why?
Always the song is—why?

Within the stone a stone
Within the frog bare bone
And the cows with their crowns
All shorn
And the sweet grass all
Green gone
And the wire's thin voice
Alone.

THERAPY 1
(I AM SUMMER)

It's the little itchy-titchy bits
That scripple on the floor,
The little itchy-titchy bits that
Scripple at the door.

My neighbour points and laughs at me,
He thinks that free for me
Will never be, "The peaks
You'll never see," says he.

"No need for me to try," say I,
"I have the luminous eye."
"I am Summer, just close by,
I am balance, space and sky."

It's the little itchy-titchy bits. . . .

We cry. We cannot fly.

This and the following five poems deal with my stay in
Northampton Mental Hospital during the 1970s.

THERAPY 2

Out to catch the garden
Hunching to its dark,
Spy the leeching moon
Graze woody throats.

Back to the room within a room,
The sullen blood, the silent notes.

Private spaces once alert
Surround the hopeless beds.
Unable now to chase the bee
Exotics lie inert,

14

Old dreams are murmured round the hive
They dream of "Rose" or "Bert".

I fold them in my breath,
I dare not bathe their brows,
No pity should disturb
Such cradle-songs of death.

THERAPY 3

When I was in the hall of fractured dreams,
and cures ran down the wires of hope in tiny,
trembling beads, bright rainbow glints of souls
were sometimes seen.

The black-bark trees stood golden in the winter
sun, my landscape yearned for sap and texture,
longed for clasping earth, my ancient head
on icy glass.

In Summer things seemed worse, vibrations purred
in shiny hum with none to know who sent them
or decode them, dead needle eyes caressing
taking notes.

Anarchic and unearthed, I screw my fortitude
to travel on the needle's kiss. I climb
another wall.

Drifting like gas he was
Dapper. He was Dapper Dan,
The one I can't forget
From whipping times.
The winds teased out to tails . . .

Unskilled figure, ludicrous
As life, slipping his
Absurdities to all.
Gritting oily silences,
Cursing closing doors.

A fizzed grenade, he shines
In incandescent rage,
Primed to blast his age,
His undiscovered days:
To self destruct.

A ragman flopped in reason's
Cage, the hours are swept
In circles, sun and shade
Repulsed, humility
A dust to cover clues.

Below the waves, things stir.
This crab begins to tire
Of silly shells, determines
Now to breathe the air,
To walk the lands, to blush—
Confer with strangers.

OCTOBER RITUALS

Like spiders, gardeners scuttle at a tremble,
worrying living things to death, working,
burning hours of work.

The bugs doing time on death-row webs, themselves
beyond their time. In the abattoires of Autumn
the torn leaves are bled.

The moon lies pretty, skidding fingernailed
across the sky, fruit lies boxed, shouts
hang on strings.

Old hopes are peeved, slow greyhounds shiver,
spades are oiled, new kindling bundled up
all tight, all staunch, for Winter.
I remember.

THE GURU

"You've altered it again,"
said the master.
"You've altered it again,
—just for fun?"

"I was bored."

"Well, you're young.
But the children crying
at the window, eh,
bit jejune, eh, bit jejune.

"Still, the bitterness
I don't mind at all, no,
I don't mind bitterness a bit.
Hang on to bitterness."

"Yes, I will."

SOURCES

A tremor in the cemetery,
Cracks break up the paths,
The blood lines laid down long
To guide me slap to mirror.

galashiels to cambuslang
auchinleck to dallas,
wanlockhead to carnwath
to galston, tain, carstairs.

More and more the dark lines crease
On busy, bird-bone hands,
Stealing silver from the river,
Teasing finesse into stone.

I contemplate the silhouettes,
The sadness in the moss.
I keen the stained dishonours,
I mourn the bright flowers mingling,
Laid all rainy in the wet.

REGRET

Black eyes in the garden, brilliant
In their gaze, across the inching day
Our memories writhe.

Held high posts in London once,
Swooped on Pathe News, sister
Pecked accordingly, of course.

This high-sky goddess faded now:
Topsy-turvy, past or present,
Silver screens corrode.

Old names misnamed, old vices claimed,
In the dust of things put down, I could
Not face old, old rapacities.

My agitation grew. In long
Slow, ticks of time old vices neatly
Drilled, old virtues nearly killed.

The hedges creaked and died.
She gazed at centuries. I had to go.
As anyone she named I was a loss.

MISS BROWN
DE CLARE

It was the war and people
Kept quite busy remembering
Who they were or what they'd
Been. Those who couldn't sat
Like anthracite, perceived to be
A nuisance or a tragedy; visiting
Seemed fine.

She sat cocooned and gaunt
Within her metal chair, which
Snared existence she defended
With a brightness and a distance.
Just beyond control her hands,
Her fingers trembling like
The sea.

Home Service radio tones—
"Thenks awf'lly too kaind".
Beyond her comfort some
Unyielding spark kept flicking
Me away, compassion held at
Bay, her smile a bright-ringed
Warning.

A savage Winter cracked with
Gnawing teeth. It bit Miss Brown
de Clare and iced her in her chair,
The stone pig on her lap as cold
As life can be, or death. For days
She sat enshrined in new despair.

THE LEGACY

This age finds sweetmeats, ruby reds, bouquets
Or bitter wines all poor persuaders.
Steel knuckles give salute.
Barbaric ways now open guts as dialogues
Yield reluctantly.
Essential give and take means someone has to lie,
To spy beneath the eaves,
Count shiny tables, varnished faces hovering,
Take subtle notes.
Now new gods in their knuckles and their cups,
Cocooned in squally violence,
Have none of that conceit which splits a man
With courtesy.
So many shipwrecks rusting on the hills;
Such beaching of civilities.
The chemist sees the mirror bones distort
A leering face.
It's all in the twist within. A random star:
A fragrance in a glass.

FOUR WORLDS

The sun was drying the first length of day
When in the wet, when in the wet
Crystals and beads stood Christ in cobwebbed stone—
             All smuggled past the cockerel.

Just beyond Him through the stitching
Undergrowth a glimpse of cattle, a glimpse
Of cattle steaming, drowned in beltedness and milk—
             All smuggled past the cockerel.

Four worlds spun in the bowl of sky and mossy trees.

First was between the cattle and the sky;
Second between the cobwebbed trees and sun;
Third was attendance round the riven stone;
Fourth I was absent at the cinema
Where there was war and carnage and grainy, grey obscenity.
             All smuggled past the cockerel.

This was occasioned during the Second World War when
cinema going and Pathe News were regular features of my
life. The statue of Christ was carved on a rock in a wild
place inaccessible to all but small, wild boys. The legend
was that a journeyman had carved it after his young
daughter died.

DEER

Through cobwebbed woods
Owls swab the air as stags
Arrive on stilts,

Patrol the fence
In flint-thin leniency,
Hind troubled.

Between the hooves
And skulls the surging
Blood exhilarates,

Spun-away from
Unicorns some say,
Birthing ruby genes.

Disorder folds
The herd like silk
In secret draws.

Ensnared in caves,
They dazzle out
Like ice-melt on the marsh.

GULLS

High up among the prisms,
The bitten into dust refracts
The cold, white snow of gulls.

Fast forward optics, heads askance,
Balances and futures soar
Superior to all.

Stitching far horizons
To their rims, cutting membranes
From the moon.

They watch the climber bounce and spin
Then voiding fixed distaste of gulls
For all things human—spit.

And where the body lies and dies
Unknown the sea-thrift crushed will grow
Through bone again

While crimsoned sunsets flay the gulls
Through murderous seas.

RUMINANT

The large and heavy pewter cow
Playing book-end to her kine
Lay down.

The weighty shiftings of a billion
Years collapsed her foggy sacking
And her shade.

Around her sweet, green fumaroles
Of Fife, old traces of funebrial
Geometry.

Her inward gaze saw oceans swelled
With clover, slick rutting deep
In byres,

The wavy, blackened tide being laid
Beside the cup marks and the silent,
Gritted castles.

FREEWILL

Do not forsake the old men
Shaking their anger at you.
Did you run from the black woods,
Their thrashing when North winds blew?
Theirs was the age that was golden
They had the courage that flew,
Theirs was the age that was true.

Do not forsake the young men
Shaking their anger at you,
They have your urge to burn forests at will,
Their obsession is yours to follow the kill.
They're living the age that is golden,
They're living your wisdoms anew.
Don't now encircle the bold,
Make promises just out of reach,
Re-invent, talk of save, talk of teach.

REFLECTIONS

The chemist in the mirror stares,
Not an image of myself —
No chemist me,

I race in airy jungles hunting
Artless, fluttering words to pin —
Assassin me.

He is riven, constancy
Unsure, his data and instructions
All to prove.

Words are fickle prey, they burn
Much deeper down than lasers may;
Raze cities.

Bite harder than the crucible,
A strict herd management in flocks
Must be observed.

Ungoverned they can menace,
Infectious, kill the killer,
Sentence judges.

We should remember words are mirrors,
Curvatures may prove endemic,
Mark my words.

With diligence, he may find gene-wrung
Formulae, star-bright codes
For old vacuums,

We both progress the butterfly way,
Osmosis is our faith; we pray
Together for the cabbages.

28

LONG VIEW

The child's gate standing
At the far end of the lawn
Had kindled old deficiencies,
Framed up much neglect.

Seen through the gate the loch
Beyond now beckoned, floating
Old resentments, reprehensions
Long forgotten.

That night the child that roams
Through old men's skulls crouched
Listening to remembered dogs
That fret in empty rooms.

He risked a bone in hardest starlight
Bringing the gate indoors and weighed
Then crushed it in his hand; slapping
Of the loch the only sound.

THINGS ATHWART

I have no dialogue with bones,
Pity drifts while wonder stares
Unfocussed with no descant in
The gut. In situ, in the cave,
It is the casal heft, the crazy
Slant of things that brings a thrilling
                                    frailty.

The moted light oblique, the sudden
Angled mass of roof, the steady
Drip as mountains mourn the small
Deaths stilled within their wombs,
Or ravished by the fire from Beaker
Folk new lit then quickly doused,
                                    alarmed.

The bones shave off their secrets as
The dying carbon bids but were
They fleshed just slightly out of true
I'd welcome the askew. Curdling
My bones sometimes the marrow rings
At what the past has brought, tomorrow
                                    brings.

SAD TALE

He sipped my throat
He sipped my knee
He sipped the secret gold from me.
His silver glances
Told me true
That this was what we had to do.
He left me space
He left me light
He scattered treasure through the night.
Then wine was spilled
The jewels gone
The rainbow ran off with the sun.

Lurking by the privet hedge
With green leaves turning brown,
The jewels still lie within the leaf
From Springtime's hateful crown,
And in my quiet and tasteful rooms
An endless burning yet consumes.

THIN COMMITMENT

From the summit in the sun,
Looking down to see her languid
On the platform by the train,
He'd understood.

Such distance was required
To view her pout, the thinness
Of her attitudes, her stance,
Her skin.

Vulnerability is tyrannous but
For him escape was possible
Unless ensnared by curvier dreams
Or lies.

Contrary-wise, her thinness was
The home he'd loved, with all his
Furniture adapted; uneasy though
That closer views

Would leave him pondering the speed
From far enchantment on the hill
To close detachment on the street.

THE KILLING YARD

Brushed by the siskin's wing
The stone walls glowed all pink
And brown, all lollygag and lazy,
Even soldier lupins swooned.

The withered farmer at the gate-lean
Distrusting softness, who knows why,
Assured me—there he'd smashed
His last horse with a hammer.

I looked ashamed for both of us.

Tough as nuts, orange-umber in
His eye, sand salted to his jowls;
Surreal old man, bizarre old death,
This morning—Eden everywhere.

He grinned his innocence.

God, what terrors old men bring
With hammers and colossal swings
Of ignorance.

CAMOUFLAGE

Kin brought me to a pied-à-terre,
Hitherto a bothy. Brass things
Abound, from fretted curbs to
Farthing bikes, a dried nut bolus
For the bay! All the walls
A sunny rage of fashion, undead,
Like me, a rufus moth sits close
Attending dusk.

The young bridge sea and sky,
Raunch up their loins and spit,
Ignoring old men crouched
In too large shirts and chairs.
Quite right!
Horizons stretch from farthing
Bikes to unimagined
Futures—mine, pray God,
'Til Christmas.

The moth and I avoid
The bothy wife and grieve,
The yellow walls, the obvious—
We leave. Necessity
Required a tasteful move.
Hope remains.

AGAINST PREVAILING WINDS

Butting his way to the West wind's walls,
A time-lapsed, stoic shell man.
Jaw clenched towards the long boats,
He longs for Spring to brush
The land and let him trace the wild flower
Stems with due care and precision.
He knows the sources of such things;
He is not weakened by finesse.

It is dead echelons of shopping
Malls, dead reels of cinema,
Dead hiss of radio, spaces
Slipped through bones and brilliant
Violences that knell. What source?
His every hour a minute rushed,
His oldest hungers starved, he dreams
Of disappearing on the tide.

High blue days dismiss such dirge
As old men's shivers, hopeless
Plain song or neglected
Cries for love but filigrees
Of Winter cannot be ignored,
Starring the homeward paths,
Smashing the old roads North.
He scans the shore for ice.

PAST FUTURES

Young decrepit flies are all around
The house, they keep appearing way before
Their season. Unsteady on their wings what trick
Produced them? What giddy elements?
What nervous fashion?

Like Gods at human windows, they don't stay long,
But blind they hit the glass, their clockwork deaths
Rejoiced by most 'though tinged with sad distaste.
A necessary waste!

WINTER'S GRIP

A dark, dark, downwind of a night
All down the chimneys round the scattering
Leaves; a night for pondering all
The unresolved, untended lairs
Where old ones lie in undetermined
States uneased by tawny pouncings
Much too late to guide.

Yet in the blasts and torn castles
Of their time, unquestionably
Flared a spark before it died
And doused prodigiously in some
Half-conquered clime. Why cannot wisdom
Every conquer age but slide
Reluctantly to leave the oldest
Fools? I once had faith in grave
And sage now only names and hopeless
Fungus rules.

THE APPRENTICE

The world held its breath
For the boy with the gun,
His twelve years swung
Between pendulum scything
Of blue-green grass and quick, starling-chattering sun.

The gun slowly spun,
Then wavered, then swung
Round the steely-braced glint of his grin
To the flower-hiding girls
Darting, spinning, giggling for fun.

Power memories focussed
Too long (a filmed waistcoat rose,
Blood-stains on a blouse) the curses
That bit like blackberry juice
And smothered and gagged in his throat in the house.

Things young or old
And those too old,
Who stood in his way
Were sighted along the sun,
Rolled round the rim of the gun, for fun.

Enhancing exclusion,
Grotesque scales against him,
Fulfilling his peaceful potential,
He targets the doves
As they float from their wrists,
Deaf to the song of the thrush in the mist.

FROZEN MOMENTS

And sometimes in that space, mid-swing
                              as it were,
It is difficult to separate realities,
                              they crowd in.
They are frightening so I count them: I note
                              the bark,
The twigs, the quality of light, distances,
                              the list is
Inexhaustible but compulsive. All this
                              can be contained,
Coped with in mid-swing; you have departed
                              not yet arrived,
Everything will change, problems will arise,
                              the only solace
Self-congratulation at the leaving. Yet still
                              that mid-swing
Moment held forever, paused and poised,
                              frozen for the
Inner eye that stares at distance hung eternally.

The miracle that amongst the details and
                              the counting,
In all our frozen moments, we can pocket
                              thawing moons
And speed them into futures full of drama
                              and new swings
Of enlightenment—not forgetting how we were,
                              the forward hunch,
The tilted head, the inward focus first.
                              A swing away,
The strength of cultured, simian grasp,
                              —the sobbing,
The tearing of the grasp, the plunge, the plunging
                              and the sobbing.

FLAT RATES

In the brick shell of this flat
Invention goes a-wandering,
Smacks the too-close walls
And squeaks; neither pacing,
Screaming, nor hurling at a
Ravished stove will compensate.

Years ago I can recall
Those sunny days of jade and
Scarlet claws, rough growling
In the boskage, when lion limbs
Would straddle gales around the globe.
Whole butcher's trays were scoffed,
Gullet stuffed like rubbish carts,

Now State bulldogs pin me here
Among the sweet-pea forty fives,
The vat that's never filled. Sweet blue
Notes sound from nests above.
A cockroach swings. I refold stressed-
Out sweaters, desperate to pluck
The apple round, to cheat the worm.

THREE NEW ZEALAND POEMS

NIGHT CREEK

Trickling down, this creek,
This sullen, yellow, way down
Through my sleep; it shivers
The room with its hanging trees
Its scattered bones and shells.

It thrashes away at the Reason
Tree, at Hermit crabs
On Flounder's bones, cut paws
On running dogs, a bandage
Coiled in sulphurate wind:

Unclassifiable,
Never quite a nightmare,
At dawn it bumped away
Uncouth as a three-legged calf.
All this in A.A. recommended.

WHAT STEAL?
(MAORI GRAVE IN ROTORUA)

The real pace of time is on them
Time to smell the flowers, steal
The flowers. What steal? Whose
Flowers? Which time?

Death of a blossom. Death in
The tribe. Time is a daffodil.
A daffodil is. We must welcome
This steal. What steal?

40

BILLY BOY

The moaning of the mad bad
Moon drove Billy Boy to sleep
Most nights but sometimes on
The really yellow nights he'd
Walk the shadowed edges bathing
In their darkness just for cleansing,
He said, but not one soul inside
Himself believed him. Truth was
Billy Boy was lost and bruised,
Adrift from rain-washed ciggy butts
To inner thigh desires, to yellow
Sand-sucked pools he used to slice
Away his days.

Time slipped off like oceans
Through his toes, wet darkness
Shot his dawns, small stuff
But balm for bully days, those ragged
Hours he did his best to keep stitched
Up and tidy. Days dreamed along
The sun's path were his best, hot driving
To the Innocent who did it for a Kindness.
Like mercury, he walked dark fragrancies
In starlit streets, compact as a can o' coke,
Yet worried people sensed the slippage
Of his mind.

His finger holds on daylight slipped
Beneath bright waterfalls and ferns.
His blood washed through the dark
Stained water, under his shades volcanoes
Ran and spent. He counted all his assets,
His privileges—like hiding in the night
Or running the hard roads out of town
Away from new brutalities. In the whiteness
Of his days he waited for his yellow moons
To guide him.

"Billy Boy" was a mentally disturbed Maori boy I met in a
coffee bar.

41

DEALER

As he slips down through the city
(Dimming the eyes, shading the days)
Houses float on the ring-bright roads,
Bouncing along on the sun's last rays.

Powdering dreams for tropic Fulham
(Kissing the needle, shining the blade)
Disability's no problem,
See all the blind folk on parade.

Conduits opening out forever,
(Channeling rainbows, filtering musk)
Sleeves unravel the falling days,
Bitter the dawn brilliant the dusk.

CYNIC

If you want to help
If you want to care
With twist and turn
And tantrum, beware,
You must not forget
If no-one's there, to cry for the empty space.

If you want to love
If love's in doubt
With twist and turn
And silence and shout,
You must not forget
If no-one's about, to cry for the empty space.

If you want to live
If the spirit's thin
With twist and turn
And stillness and spin,
You must not forget
If no-one's within, to cry for the empty space.

If it's time to die
If it's time to grieve
With twist and turn
And sigh and heave,
You must never think
You must never believe, they'll cry for the empty space.

VARIETY

Not an obvious talent, the distal,
As they say, one 'anded jugglin'
Wiv the balls below the blanket,
So to speak. 'Arry never mentioned it
Bein' only concerned wiv dexterity
Of wrist, an' floggin' insurance.

This 'Arry, modelled 'imself on 'Oudini
'Arry, who could breathe Under-Water
So they said, cunnin'ly disguised Gills
They thought. Well, this 'Arry 'ad none
O' that, just tryin' to flog insurance
'Oldin 'is breath like.

Steel balls, they were, tiny balls
Between the fingers rollin' them
Over, under, through, because a
Second talent could be vital
Come the crash, another string,
'E reckoned, "Variety" maybe.

'E even practised in the bath, thinkin'
Underwater would be good but
It wasn't an' 'e drowned, wiv eight
Steel balls embedded in a Swollen
Gesture, too thick to roll now,
Or even float.

See, in Variety, on the stage, or even
In the wings, a punter out o' work
'Olds 'is breath, rolls wiv the balls
An' if the routine's rubbish, dies the
Death. That's how it is if you perform,
Ask any Tom or Dick.

SEEKING WEST

Anger begins;
Inadequate, muzzled to growl,
Deep in convention's cage afraid
To bite, afraid to speak,
Reduced to slinging grapeshot at
The sea with all its slimy,
Swimmy things. Sometimes this anger
Channels laser-like
With keen finesse to crisp the un-
Suspecting dunes to glass.

I wish to praise unsubtle things;
Big, blousy close-ups are
My need. I seek the rose, whiles kill
For fresh, green overgrowth
Or hill, this old mole travelling round
Trepanned and circling nowhere,
Blind, in careless, tumbling sand.

THE OPTIMIST

Now I feel all sadnesses
within me and they are
not so very old.

Just recently when young
and strong at the jumping
and the running and the
singing, not for one atom
of a second did I believe
anyone was better.
No hedge could be so high
but I would soar. On a
standing start neither wind
nor cheetah could live
in my gale. My voice was
sweeter than any known
to nightingales.

This was so.
No doubt.
In my fibres.

Looked at another way
my running was geometrically
co-ordinated to the Nth degree.
My jumping had deer hirpled
in my wake. My singing dinged
and donged down cliffs.

This was so.
No doubt.
In my fibres.

So why feel all the sadnesses
within when they are
not so very old?

Well, recently,
the jumping and the running
and the singing have declined,
--in truth—decrepit.

This is so.
No doubt.
In my fibres.

Looked at another way
my sadnesses are HUGE
profundities. Great DRAMAS
for the Gods.

This is so.
No doubt.
In my fibres.

CAT'S -PAW

Each old rubbish bag of city
Tips out its starry waste
In the swirly, salty seas and through
This like a thrown stone dropped
The plane.

The Gods at play.

At birth they exchange the foetus cord for Time.
Time necklace starts its slow life's work.
The Gods are laughing, we have become the Gods'
Umbilicus. Time is their afterbirth. They allow
Us to dig an ultramundane grave.

COWBOY STAR

Wyatt Earp was in telescopes,
Earp junior that is, as was,
Earp senior the well-known cowboy
Having shot to celestial applause.

Earp junior compressed, refracted
All he knew in holes,
Earp senior decreased, compacted
As syrup for the moles.

Earp junior researched him to nothing;
Matter far too dense for souls.

REMEMBERED BEEB

Lost in a familiar place throwing
Names like pebbles down a well. From
The canteen seeking "Highgate Tom" who once
Assured security and compassed North.
All the names remembered smeared like flies
Across a glass.

I listen to the hum.

There seems no naughtiness, no ribaldry,
Perhaps they're lured to ancient discs, forced
To worship old hyperboles or razored
By sharp memos born of fear. I force
Down cold collations marvelling at gargantuan
Appetites of public service; such fine waste
Thrown away.

"Highgate Tom" is a church on the skyline directly North as seen
from the BBC canteen.

AN OLD
THESPIAN
PREPARES

After showering
I am quiet and
wise and strong.
Clothes sit easy
on me.
Sins remain but
not for long.
Problems melt
before my gaze.
I scythe through
traffic, through
the maze
to Hampstead,
Arch of Marble,
Hyde Park Corner
then The Court.
Madmen bare
their fangs
at fenders,
rubber squeals,
glass retorts.
Nothing impinges —
EVERYTHING impinges
(I'll use it).
Theatre's my skin.
All will be well

BEGIN!

EARLY START

So wee they wur, an' close,
Wan fist o' shadow cast
Them baith, wan-legged camels,
Triple toe-loops, a' the gear.

But yon's the age compulsions
Must be cairried oot.
Wee Torvill grabs wee Dean
An' birls, an' skites him doon
The ice a' bum an' bits.

Thir's auld yins gaun aboot
That's jist the same.—A'
Mid-week the caird's no merked
But perfect sixes aye drawn oot
Oan Sundays. Aye, yer maw!

FRAGMENTS

Alternatives were tae haun',
Still ma faither aye chose
The kindest route, the wan that offered nonsense.

We never kent his stars, his sky,
Nor sensed his climb tae duties efter tea,
Yet Mither's star it wiz that drew him oan.

And we followed tae a view
O' distant hills and possibilities,
Gey often tummlin', dizzy, 'en famille'
      tae bounce

And prowl the hill-fit singin'
Tae the wind, bar Sundays 'coorse. Blythe
Faither frae the rhubarb-pungent gairden

Smilin', sensuous oan the earth-tramp
O' auld boots, a swoonin' swallow captured
In his fist, aye perky—never feart.

Never feart o' onythin', my Faither,
Efter Ypres unhinged a' futures, chinged
The players or, as ma Faither thocht, chinged
      the gemme.

. . .

That nicht the world upended,
Familiar, fixed things slid.
A marble clock, a frieze,
A marbled sea, an' me,
Time wintert, hidin' 'til
The thaw.

The wire-thin thickness o'
Ma Faither's pulse, fuse thin
Through unhelt days; baby-
Soor, sweet sickness, poalish.
His breath, a whispering thief,
Rins in an' oot each day;

The day gangs dreich. I long
For brassy things, cauld windae
Panes that cut.

Bells ring, stirrin's occur.
He bides.
His hair relaxin' noo,
Lost in the ward—blue licht.

HERTS 'N' ROSES

Mebbe love's been o'er rough,
O'er mony cuts too near the quick
But somethin' in yon fu'-blawn rose
Pinned b' the gairdner tae the rid-grey wa',
Cries back ma mind tae sma' deceits.

When damage has been hid o'er lang,
There's no much dignity occurs
Frae stakin' up a rose or hert
Tae feenish a' its days in Winter
Snaw. Faur better cut or burnt.

AULD NICK ABUNE

For a' tae view
His doon-wind hing
Gies bield* tae a'.   shelter
Gif we could hing lik' thon
—Avaunt the gress.

He ower-hings
A thoosand deeps.
Ahint his een
Glowers great stramash,* oor sair   rumpus
Forfochten* warld.   worn out

His lineage hings
Aff breist-bane rid,
His neb* an' claws   nose (beak)
Wi' ran-dan* bluid aye clagged,*   roistering, clogged
Yet wi' rumgumption*   commonsense

Tholes* yon coinage o'   bears
Bad cess*, the cleck*   tax, the chatter
Ablow. Whaur mair
Ha'e less—is thirled*—is his;   obligated
Whaur raggy chiels

Stravaig* in crimson   wander
Snaw—is his;
Nor yet transgressor,
Nor transgressed, he kens
Nae fealty steys:*   loyalty stays

An' kens for'by
He's faur abune*   far above
Sic debts, an' same-
Wey kens thir skirlin'* cannae   shrieking
Rummle* him.   upset

54

AULD NICK ABLOW

Grat eeriness o' oceans ring
Blue sadnesses o' whales, whoopin
Lang loops o' loss an moornin' doon
The swell.

Men fash* themsels oan killin' boards,   vex
Rid-rory tae thir thrapples* for   throats
Glit* greed.   slimy

They jaunder* th' explosion's quick,   talk jokingly
They jaunder that nae sea can speak,
But by guid Christ it greets,
Blirtin' ablow the hush mune's loof[1]
Slidderin* roon the wynds.   Slithering

Beyont a' nature, forbye a' creeds,
In some lang time'll soond a race-thocht
O' a weetness, a strang scream-bellied
Agony, a warnin' o' vile evil
Filterin' doon.

[1] Weeping below the rushing moon's foot.

55

WEE
ANDY BRITAIN

Wee Andy Britain
had a top lip grey
or green or carmine,
the rest was under wraps.

ICE PANTOMIME

Tilts

Thrusts

Indiscreet discretions

Glides

Scrapes

Obsolete progressions

Clutches of harmony

Slithering over pins

Smiles like broken icicles

Everybody wins

"BOGEY" HITS
CAM'SLANG

Oor lot stood for decency
Hauf heeelan', hauf wee-free,
An' trustin' only them wi'
Bowler hats an' collars.

I blame the other truth,
'Specially at week-ends
When I was five-fingered Louie,
In the rain, snarlin'

At empty dugs, astonished
Tae find a schoolboy, Canis
Familiaris. Later, before
Vinegar or salt were shook

I'd murdered seventeen in the
Battered "chippy" where haddocks
Fried black puddin's jist fur laughs.
Molls were scarce but on the corner,

Auld Sadie sellin' football's
Crazy, broken dreams . . .
Yeah, she could be moulded—
Things would be taken care of!

Anyway, they took what they got
An' what they got was pilot,
Hired gun, rodeo rider, best freen,
Horn man an' a Saturday zombie,

An' once nearly, my hand
Up Maisie's guernsey, but I was
Away, bouncin' an' bumpin', an' eatin'
Carmen Miranda's hat—no sweat.

Oot there in the minin' sumps
The collier's sowl* gets burnt,   soul
That hackin' cough, that smoorin' dross,* smothering coal-
That heids a dollar at pitch an' toss,   dust
Strippin' the shadows aff the wa's
In Ayrshire's diamond ha's.

O'er love, an' birth, an' strife,
That blightin' rage o'er life,
Lancin' again at man an' wife:
The rattlin' fa' o' rattlin' braith,
Burnin' the boxes bocht* tae gie folk   bought
Decency in daith.

Up an' doon lik' fuckin' yo-yos
Dancin' oan a tumshie* string,   turnip
Well fuck yer sangs, an' fuck yer crack,
Thir nae bliddy guid, thir jist the slack
Tae damp doon the dander* o' folk oan the rack,   anger
An' a'body kens bar the man at the tap
This wasnae the sang at yer Mither's pap.

AUCHINLECK
INHERITANCE

When I was nearly three thir seemed
Nae end tae space, the huge unknown.
A joy tae struggle oot, tae tadpole
Frae the spawn.

Thir was singin' frae the trees
An' dancin' in the rainbow rains
An' colours smelled that guid 'n' tert
When glitterin' through tobacca stains:
An' a' that coonted.*   counted

An' ah wiz Don Quixotey, breathless,
Chergin' through the rhubarb beds,
White coffins passed me doon the brae,
While batmen chased me roon the sheds:
An' a' that coonted.

But faces pinched inside their skin
New drawn in frae the death next door.
Frae bungled pits the black-daurk stunk,
An' mair the free-drawn space closed in,
A' roon the Ayrshir' hedges shrunk:
An' a' that coonted.

An' then they tellt us;
"Wan fur the leerie,* an' wan fur the ma't   lamplighter
An' wan fur the pepper, an' wan fur the sa't
An' wan tae go, an' wan tae stay
An wan tae go doon the steep, rid brae",*   red hill
An' a' that coonted.

EAST NEUK

This huddle wracked aboot
But tidy—some hooses there
Wi' blindet een* tae hide   blinded eyes
Stramash* or see aff strangers.   trouble

A man can bide inside
The kernel o' the corner
Winds, an' skliff braced up
Tae sniff the sixpenny sea—
Breathcatchin' whiles.

A ticht turf keeps things ticht,
But cacklers at the cemeteries,
The slee-slung gulls, scream
Oot the heroes, a' the shilpit* an'   thin and insipid
The obdurate shauchlin'* through   shuffling
Dead drunk an' roarin' fu'

Hard bitten rocks still bite,
An' auld yins that have seen
The hale thing backyairds sine*   since
Stane coffins oan the Fisher
Dykes, gang cleekin'* oot   hooking
The partins,* hard as hell,   crabs
Yet lichtsome whiles, lik'
Weasels dancin'.

When ah hung masel' in the wardrop
An' brushed away the oose, *   fluff
The suit sashays doon the ster an' parks,
Appropriate as ye like in—"The Blue Room".

A rid dress wi' a frizz o' yella*   yellow
Comes oan familiar.
"Lookin' fur Action," it says, lik' a
Crazy, mixed up predatory mop.

"Depends whit kind,
"Ah've jist unfoldit, travel staint, y'know."

"Ye huv yer pick," says Big Moppet.
"action action
quiet action
middle action
gentle action
nae action
maddy action
depresst action."

Says me,
"naw, naw, haw, nain o' thaim. *   none of those
The suit's blue, y'know,
v'ye got peace?"

"Yeah, peace ah can dae," says rid froack
"—but, strictly, only efter action."

So blue suit gave
Rid dress a wee press,
Then they baith jist
Crumpilt* in the coarner.   crumpled

NIGHT OWLS

Only owls have wisdom, only owls are wise,
Some birds amend with bright rear ends
And peacocks have their eyes,
But only owls keep silence, only owls keep shtumm,
The rest in parks indulge in larks
But only owls keep mumm.
Some song-birds hit the high notes,
Some wrens betray their size,
But only owls by darkness steer and see through one's
disguise,
So owls have great sagacity, at work, at rest, at play
Incredibly bright throughout the night,
They're knackered through the day.

ANCIENT AND MODERN

The sea roared the pebble sucked
The lapwing tumbled the penguin way
The moon threw down some cucumber bones,
Offcuts from sleeves of the sea.

All were buoyed on the razorbill tide
Then flounced on the thread of a lark.
On the rim of the sea, the rim of a thistle,
The rim of the moon, the silvery dark,
Bounced on the bones of a lark.

The stonechat rattled the gourd on the tree
The stonechat ratttled the band.
The plovers whispered the words to the sea,
The song of the words as fish kissed the land,
This is the song for me.

Once, in youth, a different song,
A song of the birches silver and blue,
Silver and blue the twins of the sea
My loves they were and green they grew.

They grew the shade for the bird of woe
To hide in the bush, the woven bush,
To open and close in the summer slow,
The bird of woe in silver and black
Impaling the ancients on thorny rack
When the birch tree fell, the shrike flew back.

A song was sung of tender night
A wrung blue sky a fox delight
A fingerling posing all of the night
On a reed of umber and rose—in water
Brackish, comatose, water still and slow.

Two songs to sing, always to learn
Two places to live, to die and be born,
To die and be born but never to know,
Two songs to learn but never to know.

LAPIS LAZULI

A lapis lazuli long, long lizard
Lay on a layer of aquamarine
On a ledge, with a scarlet gizzard,
The only location such lizards are seen.

He'd not been murdered,
Not been raped.
The dust of learning,
He'd escaped.

He'd not been slandered,
Not been sued.
Never been questioned,
No-one was rude.

People imagined he must have expired
But no, he'd been thinking and simply felt tired,
You might think it's wearing for lizards so blue
But they wouldn't be happy as lapis.

DAURK WHISTLE

Ah aye had the feelin'
Daunerin'* roon the blue cage   strolling aimlessly
That ah wiz oot
An' a' the rest wur in.
Inside thir ain wee boaxes,
Jumpin' oot tae say "Hullo",
An' ah'm ootside cryin' in
"Hullo"
But jist tae naebody, ye ken.

Then whiles, thir wiz a shift
An' a' things vicey-versa.

A' the rest wir oan
The ootside lookin' in,
An' cryin' "Hullo"
An ah wiz oan the inside
Lookin' oot an' cryin' . . .

An' feart at times that
Lids o' boaxes snag.

It wid be nice nae boaxes, eh?
Coorse, if it wiz easy
As a' that, the warld'd still
Be flat, nae doot.
Mebbe no' sae mony boaxes
Bar* the big yin at the last.   except

65

BAD NEEBORS

Huge he wiz, huge.
Giant auroch eye, distendit
Belly an' that wiz only
The wean;* wee Joe Goliath,   infant
Well known in the "dear green", * Glasgow
An' that; faither jist the same
Only gianter wi' nae morality.
Mrs "G", a puir sowl,* aye   poor soul
Pesterin' the neebors fur anither
Dug* tae eat, nae wunner folks dog
Wiz scunnert* but naeb'dy'd the sickened
Nous tae chinge things 'cept
Wan day wee Davie Bloomberg's
Dug wiz kicked by Joe then et* eaten
By Mrs "G", the faither jist staunin'
There an' laughin', an' wee Davie'd
Hud enough.
"Haw you," he says, "Wiz that ma dug
You jist et?" An' oan affirmation,
Picked up a V.C. pie an' skited it* threw it
Aboot a million miles up an' broke
The big yin's nose.
"Take that," he says, "an' the next wan'll
Be worser, 'cause it's gonna cost ye."
Big "G" kneeled doon tae see this
Wee pluke* that wiz itchin' 'im. wee boil
"Haw," he says, "haw you, wiz that fair
Ah wiznae ready, an' besides, wae ma
Wife an' the wean present, ah'm
Somewhit hampert."
"O.K." says the bold Bloomberg, "dae
Yez want tae buck history?"
"Aw Jesus," says big "G".
"Naw listen," says the wee man, "ah'll
Speak loud an' clear," so he spoke
Loud an' clear. "From herewith," he
Spoke clearly an' quite loud, "youz

Will skedaddle* doon tae that far Minster   run away
In the Sooth, 'll vote Tory an' will
NEVER RETURN!"—he was quite adamant.
This smitet the Goliaths coz they owed a few,*   were in debt
So they went quietly but of coorse they fixed
It an' noo they're back an' naebody's makin'
Thae pies lik' bullets any mair, an' forbye
That, they're movin' Philistines intae the
Schemes, an' ah doot wee Davie's quangoed
So the ba' is oan the slates*—irrevocably!   the game's up
Unless they let us make a lot mair pies.

CAVITY SONG

Big big big fat wumman
Big big big fat weans*   children
Huge big huge big fat man,
In the room where ye wait, where ye wait.

Big big big big terror
Drill drill drill ootbye
White white white assistant,
Face lik' a, face lik' a clamp.

Big big big big gruntin'
Wee wee wee wee squeaks
Big wumman big weans big man a' vamoosed,
Lik' grease, lik' grease, lik' grease aff a djuck.*   duck

Nice nice nice clean space
Nae nae nae nae pain
Come again come again come again,
Bye-bye. Next please.

67

ENCLOSURES

The open fields, the fields o' space
An' sunburst Seturdays tummlin'* through.   tumbling
Only oan the ticht, hoat* bed   tight, hot
Wi' daith a close thing, could somersau'ts
Lik' thon occur again.

When ah got better, a' thaim responsible
Hud plantit hedges.